Hello out there!

BODY LANGUAGE

Pam Robson
Illustrated by Colin Mier

W
FRANKLIN WATTS

A Division of Grolier Publishing
NEW YORK • LONDON • HONG KONG • SYDNEY
DANBURY, CONNECTICUT

First American Edition 1997 by
Franklin Watts, A Division of Grolier Publishing
Sherman Turnpike, Danbury, CT 06816

Robson, Pam.
    Body language / Pam Robson.
        p.   cm. -- (Hello out there!)
    Includes index.
    Summary: Considers how humans and animals use their bodies to
communicate without words.
    ISBN 0-531-14468-2
    1. Body language--Juvenile literature. 2. Animal communication-
-Juvenile literature. 3. Psychology, Comparative--Juvenile
literature. [1. Body language. 2. Animal communication.]
I. Title. II. Series.
BF637.N66R63 1997
153.6'9--dc21   97-3784
                                                               CIP
                                                               AC

Series editor: Rachel Cooke
Designer: Melissa Alaverdy
Picture research: Sarah Snashall

Printed in Belgium
Picture acknowledgments:
Cover image (background): Robert Harding (Ralph Clevenger),
all others Steve Shott.
Ancient Art and Architecture/Ronald Sheridan p. 29;
John Birdsall p. 19; Bruce Coleman pp. 11br (Dr. P. Evans), 14c
(Andy Purcell); Corbis-Bettmann p. 22; Robert Harding p. 13;
Hutchison Library p. 5 (Crispin Hughes), 27 (J.G. Fuller);
Image Bank p. 26; NHPA pp. 11bl (Gerard Lacz), 14b (Steve
Robinson); Oxford Scientific Films p. 9 (Clive Bromhall);
Rex Features pp. 17 (Sipa), 18 (Sipa), 21 (J. Sutton-Hibbert), 25;
Frank Spooner p. 6 (Gamma).

CONTENTS

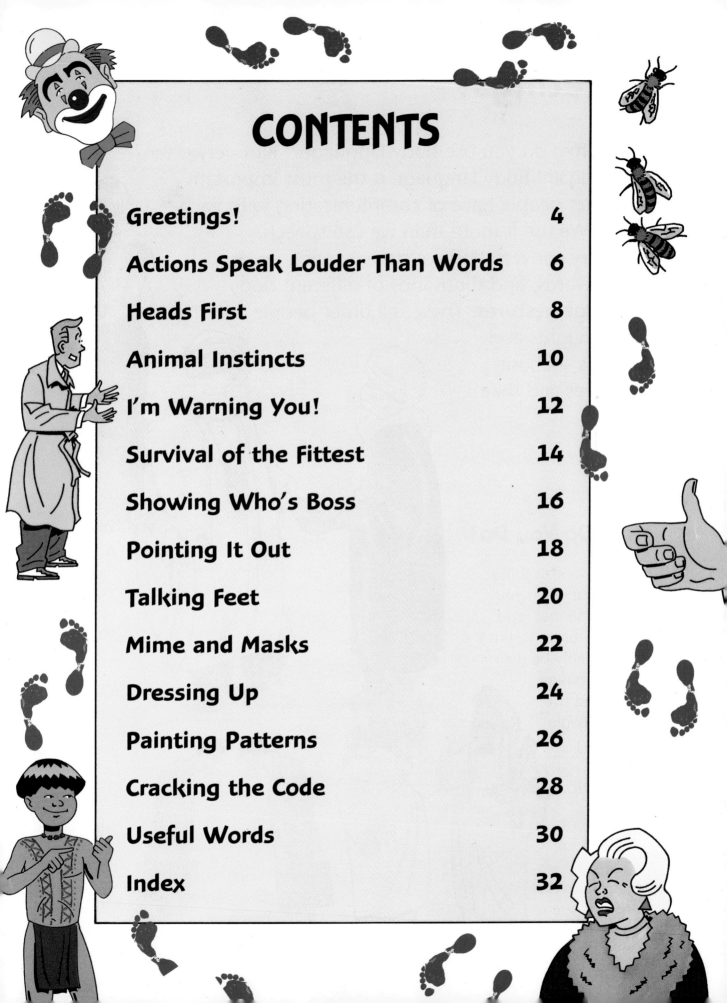

Greetings!

How often do you use body language? Not very often? Think again! Body language is the most important way that people have of communicating with each other. We use it more than we use speech.

Every conversation we have is made up of a few words, and thousands of different body language **gestures**. These tell other people our thoughts and feelings —about ourselves and them!

▲ The French use a light embrace and a hugging action on either side of the chest.

How Do You Do?

What is the first thing you notice when you meet someone? You may not realize it, but it will probably be their body language. All around the world, people are saying hello by using their bodies.

◀ The **Tuareg** in the Sahara desert lightly touch hands several times.

◀ In Japan, both people bow. There is very little eye contact. You bow deeply to someone important.

Arab **Bedouin** ▶ men stroke their beards.

4

HELLO!

The handshake started off as a way of showing someone that you were not holding a weapon. Now it is recognized throughout the world as a friendly greeting.

Egyptians kiss three times: first on one cheek, then on the other, then back on the first cheek.

▼

▲ Mexicans give one kiss on the cheek.

▲ Italians give four kisses – two on each cheek!

In Polynesia, both people lean forward and rub noses gently backwards and forwards.

▼

◄ A religious greeting in India involves putting the palms of the hands together and holding the hands in front of the body.

Actions Speak Louder Than Words

People are able to talk to each other because they have a **voicebox**—unlike other animals. But we do not all speak the same language. Perhaps the world would be a better place if we did!

There are between 2,500 and 5,000 different languages in the world, not including **dialects**. But body language has over 1 million different signals and gestures—many of them **universal**.

> **HELLO!**
> Animals may not talk but they do communicate—not only with howls and squawks but also with body language, which is often much more complex than any we use!

Getting the Message

How would you give a message to someone who doesn't speak your language? Sports referees often face this problem during games with teams from different countries. They have found a good solution in body language: a set of arm and hand signals that everyone can understand.

Referees make their signals large and obvious, so that everybody on the field and in the crowd can see them.

What Did You Say?

Many different people use universal body language signs when they are at work. In very noisy situations, it may be the only way to make yourself understood. Here are a few examples.

◀ Traffic police officers use their hands, arms, and the position of the body to tell drivers to stop.

Airport workers ▶ have signals to tell airplanes where to move around the airport.

A music conductor ▶ uses hands, arms, and facial expressions to give instructions to the musicians.

WINK!

A music conductor recently injured his arm just before a performance. He managed to direct the orchestra using only winks and nods.

I Know How You Feel!

Many of the gestures we make tell other people how we are feeling. Sometimes, these gestures are **involuntary**—we do not mean to make them.

We might smile or laugh when we are happy.

Some people blush when they are feeling embarrassed.

Our mouths turn downwards, and we might cry, when we are sad.

Frowning, or glaring, is body language for angry.

7

Heads First

Most body language starts with the face. The many different muscles work together to help us to blink, wink, nod, shake, and stare. We use 15 different muscles to smile. A frown needs more than 40! Some face signals are tiny, like raising eyebrows in surprise, or creasing the forehead when you are puzzled. Others use the whole head, like nodding to say yes, or shaking the head to say no.

HELLO!

The busiest muscles in the face are in the eyelids. They move over 20,000 times every single day.

Eye, Eye!

Our eyes are always flashing out signals about the way we are feeling. Have you ever stared angrily at somebody, or winked to show you have a secret? We often describe our moods or feelings by describing the way that our eyes look.

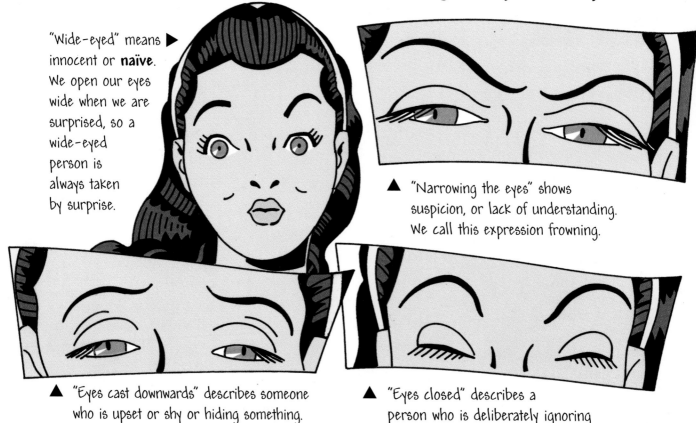

"Wide-eyed" means ▶ innocent or **naïve**. We open our eyes wide when we are surprised, so a wide-eyed person is always taken by surprise.

▲ "Narrowing the eyes" shows suspicion, or lack of understanding. We call this expression frowning.

▲ "Eyes cast downwards" describes someone who is upset or shy or hiding something. We avoid eye contact in these moods.

▲ "Eyes closed" describes a person who is deliberately ignoring something—or who may just be asleep!

Ape gape

Where do all our expressions and gestures come from? The scientist **Charles Darwin** studied the faces his baby son made in his crib and compared them with apes. He found that many were similar—although they did not necessarily mean the same thing. An ape grins, for example, not to show happiness—but fear.

Eventually Darwin decided that humans probably **evolved** from apes, and that their expressions developed into the ones we use today.

Activity:
SHORT STORY

Write a short story using words or phrases based on body language. You are not allowed to use the proper names for emotions—such as sad, happy, or **embarrassed**. Instead, describe what we do with our eyes, lips, head, and other parts of the body when we are feeling that way.

WINK!

Not all body expressions mean the same things in all parts of the world. The headshake, for example, might mean "no" in many countries—but in Turkey and Greece, "no" is signaled by throwing the head backwards.

9

Animal Instincts

Animals may not be able to talk, but they use their mouths and their faces to communicate by body language. Their faces become little signaling machines, flashing messages to one another.

Ear, Ear

Human ears are not very useful for sending messages. But many animals can do all sorts of exciting things with theirs! Look at this dog. Can you see how it uses its ears to show what it is thinking?

WINK!

Dogs can only learn to understand simple commands from humans such as "Sit" and "Down." Chimpanzees, on the other hand, can learn a form of sign language. One chimp, named Washoe, knew over 200 words and could "speak" complete sentences.

A Day in the Life of Barney the Dog

I'm not sure what's going on.

What's that over there?

I don't like you!

You're the boss.

Keep Away!

Animals often use face and head signals to ward off their enemies. The body language must be absolutely clear. A mistake could mean the difference between life and death.

Tigers have big white spots behind their ears. When an enemy approaches, the tiger reveals the spots to signal a warning.

Elephants hold their ears out wide to make themselves look big and threatening.

Family talk

Face signals are important for animals within family groups, too. Members of the group "read" the faces of the others to avoid trouble.

Open mouths can be a warning sign—a male baboon will yawn to expose its **canine teeth** if another male comes too close.

Or open mouths —like these baby birds'—can say "I'm hungry!"

11

I'm Warning You!

We often use body language to send out warnings to other people. Where we stand, and what we do with our bodies, all depend upon how we are feeling.

I'm Angry!

The way someone is holding their body—their **posture**—can show you whether they are in a good mood or a bad mood.

If you feel nervous you may fold your arms. But folded arms can also mean that you are angry!

This person is probably ready for an argument! Folded arms, hunched shoulders, and crossed legs provide a barrier between you and the other person—rather like building up battlements in a war.

HELLO!

Sales assistants are often taught to notice body language. They will never ask a customer to make a decision if their arms and legs are folded.

If you are in a good mood, all the defenses come down! Your head will be held up high, your arms will be hanging loose by the side of the body, and and your back will be straight.

12

You're in My Space!

We all try to keep some personal space, wherever we are. People and animals tend to use their bodies to show other people where their **territory** is.

You may "stand guard" in the doorway if you don't want someone going into your bedroom. Pulling your shoulders back and keeping your legs firmly placed makes you look bigger and stronger.

You may spread arms and elbows out across your desk to keep your working space private. This is the human way of making yourself look bigger than you are.

Party Manners

Next time you are at a party, think about personal space! The space around our bodies is part of our territory, too. If you stand too close to somebody you make them feel uncomfortable. The usual size of a "personal space zone" varies between cultures. In Japan, for example, it is acceptable to stand 10 in. (25cm) from the person you are speaking to, but Americans seem to need more space—around 18 in. (46cm).

WINK!

Standing too close to someone causes actual physical changes in their body. Their heart will pump more quickly and a chemical called **adrenaline** is released, to prepare the body to fight the "intruder" in their space.

Survival of the Fittest

Some animals have built-in body language signals. The markings and colors on their bodies send out very clear messages, which help the animal to survive.

Look at Me!

All animals produce babies. If they did not, they would soon die out. The male of the **species** is often more brightly colored than the female, and the animal will often use eye-catching body language displays to attract a mate.

The peacock displays his amazing plumage to attract a female peahen. She has only drab, brown feathers.

Some mating signs are very obvious indeed. One type of female monkey's behind becomes swollen and bright red to attract males!

Hide and Seek?

Some animals can hide from their enemies by becoming the same color as their background, so that they cannot be seen. This is called **camouflage**. Some animals' body shape also helps them hide—they look more like plants than animals!

Spot the Animal

The Bengal tiger lives in grassy or swampy areas and forests, where its stripes blend with the straight lines of the trees and plants.

The arctic hare grows a white coat in the winter, to blend in with the snow.

The leafy sea dragon is the same color and shape as pieces of floating seaweed.

I'm Dangerous!

Another good way to fool enemies is to pretend you are someone else. Animals do this all the time!

Some moths have markings like eyes on their wings to startle their enemies.

HELLO!
The male bull's-eye fish changes color according to its mood. It is silver when it is afraid, and orange when it is aggressive.

The pearl-spotted owlet has markings on the back of its head that look just like a face, to guard against attacks from behind.

Showing Who's Boss

Humans and animals often have a leader or "top dog." Have you noticed that some people seem to stand out in the crowd as "natural leaders"? People often send out body language signals to show the rest of the pack that they are in charge.

WINK!

In a colony of wasps, the leaders automatically eat the most food. The lowest ranking wasps have to fetch it for them—and build the nest!

Top Dog

Your hand gestures can be a sign of power or weakness. The handshake is a good example.

A firm handshake will make others feel that you are confident, but a floppy one will give the signal that you are weak or giving in to them.

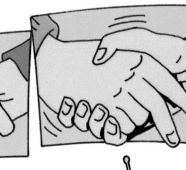

Palms say something, too: upturned, they are a begging or pleading gesture; but turned downwards, they mean that you are in control.

Who's in Charge?

In this interview, the man on the left is obviously winning the argument. He is leaning forward, keeping eye contact, and using big arm gestures. The man on the right is sitting back in his chair, crossing his legs, and looking downwards. These are all signs of weakness. Next time you watch an interview on TV, watch the body language and decide who is in charge . . .

Yes, Sir!

In the armed forces, everybody has their place above or below everyone else from new **recruits** to officers. Soldiers have to learn how to signal with their bodies—by saluting, clicking heels, or standing to attention—to show who is boss.

We sometimes use the same sort of code in everyday life. We may greet a close friend with a hug; a business colleague with a handshake; and a very important person with a bow or curtsy. The different body language signals tell the person we are meeting how friendly, or how important, they are to us.

Pecking Order

Animal leaders often use aggressive body language to show who's boss. Hens have a pecking order: the top hen in a group pecks all the other hens. The next hen in line pecks all the ones beneath her. The poor hen at the bottom is pecked by all the others!

Pointing It Out

Hands are very useful things! Humans and animals have always used them for eating, holding or grooming. But people have also learned that they can be used to send messages.

Hooray!

Sometimes we use our hands and fingers to show the world in general how we are feeling. Look at this picture of a crowd at a sports event. You can tell by the positions of the hands that this side is supporting the winning team. They are punching the air or throwing up their hands in triumph.

The supporters on the losing side might shrug their shoulders or hang their heads. But what hand signals do you think they might use?

HELLO!

Hand gestures can have different meanings in different countries. The "thumbs up," for example, means "OK" in Britain, Australia, and America; is the sign for the number one in Italy; and is very rude indeed in Greece . . .

Pointed Remarks

Other hand signals send a very clear message to one person in particular.

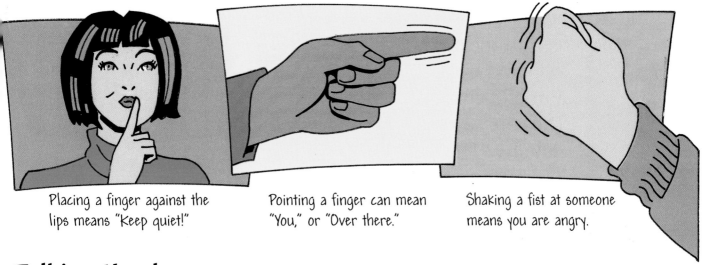

Placing a finger against the lips means "Keep quiet!"

Pointing a finger can mean "You," or "Over there."

Shaking a fist at someone means you are angry.

Talking Hands

Over two hundred years ago, a French priest called Charles de L'Epée noticed two sisters who were deaf using their hands and fingers to make signs at each other. He used their idea to invent the **deaf-dumb sign language**. As well as the hand and finger signs, this system uses exaggerated body language gestures and expressions. You show that you are asking a question by having a "questioning" look on your face.

Talking Feet

What you do with your feet can reveal a lot about you! Have you ever seen someone with their feet up on a desk or with their legs swinging over the arm of a chair? They are saying loudly: "This is my property!" If you see someone tapping a foot on the ground, they may be sending out a signal that they are feeling impatient!

Top: "This is my desk!"
Left: "Come on, hurry up!"
Bottom: "Listen to me!"

Standing Your Ground

Standing with both feet firmly balanced can help you feel confident in front of others. Have you ever had to present something to your class? If it makes you feel nervous, make sure you are firmly balanced on your feet before you begin. When you feel ready, look at the class and stand up tall. With your feet firmly in place you will feel in control.

What a Mover!

Your feet can also be instruments for dancing. When we dance at parties or in formal displays, our feet send out messages, such as "I like you," or "I'm part of the group."

Dancing feet can express joy and celebration!

Some animals dance, too. Honeybees move their bodies to tell other bees in the hive where **nectar** can be found.

If the bee dances in a circle, the nectar is close by.

A figure eight dance means it is farther away.

If the dancing bee flies upwards, it means the other bees must fly in the direction of the sun.

Once Upon a Time...

Before books and television were invented, people told stories to each other through dance. Many traditional dances are acting out folk tales, such as the Eagle Dance of the **Comanche** people, or the Australian **Aboriginal** Dance of the Wounded Seagull. Stories are still told through dance. Have you ever seen a classical ballet? The dancers use mime to show moods and feelings.

To cry

Fear

HELLO!

The stickleback fish changes color and does an elaborate zigzag dance just before the female lays her eggs.

Anger

To hide

Mime and Masks

Actors and **mime** artists are experts at using body language to entertain us. They study people's expressions and the way that they move very carefully. When a good mime artist steps through an imaginary door, the audience believes that the door really exists!

Acting Up

Actors and entertainers have to make the audience understand what they are doing and thinking by using their body language. They do this by making their movements and gestures very large and obvious—or "larger than life". If we moved like this in everyday life, we would look very silly indeed!

Activity:
BE A MIME

Take turns to mime a character, an animal, or a well-known person for the group. Can they guess who you are?

Animal Mime

Some animals use a form of mime—not for entertainment, but for protection against an enemy. Often an animal tricks a **predator** into leaving it alone.

The plover will pretend to have an injured wing to draw attention away from its nest of young.

The opossum pretends to be dead if it is threatened—"playing possum." The species has survived for 130 million years!

Behind the Mask

It is very difficult to discover how someone is feeling if you cannot see their face. In the huge outdoor theaters of Ancient Greece, the audience could not see the actors clearly. To make it quite clear what sort of character was being played, the actors wore masks.

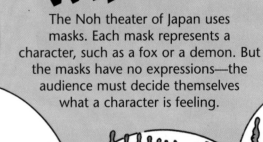

WINK!

The Noh theater of Japan uses masks. Each mask represents a character, such as a fox or a demon. But the masks have no expressions—the audience must decide themselves what a character is feeling.

The features on Greek masks were exaggerated, and specially-shaped mouth pieces made the actors' voices louder.

Dressing Up

What you wear can make a statement about you. Clothes can cover up body language, or they can exaggerate it. Some people want to be noticed. Others want to look like their friends. Many people simply want to feel comfortable in their clothes.

Look at Him!

People tend to judge others from the way they are dressed. It is very easy to make snap judgments about people from their clothing. We call this **stereotyping**.

Where do you think these people work? Do their clothes "say" something about them?

It is easy to jump to conclusions!

24

Peas in a Pod

Do you wear a uniform? Whether you wear one for school or for work, the effect is the same. A uniform shows that you are a member of a group. It can tell other people where you are from, or what you do for a living. A uniform also disguises your body language and makes you look like everyone else in the group. The word "uniform" means "alike."

Policewoman ▶

Nurse ▶

◀ Soldier

School uniforms ▶

HELLO!

Dark colored clothes—like police uniforms—make the person who is wearing them look important and official. Light clothes, on the other hand, make people feel that they can talk to you.

Part of the Crowd

Being fashionable usually means wearing the same kind of clothes as your friends. In a way, it is another kind of uniform. You are using your clothes to tell the world that you belong to a particular group. Do you like to look different or do you prefer to be part of the crowd?

25

Painting Patterns

Body language can be exaggerated by adding colors or markings to the skin. People who use body paints or **tattoos** are usually sending very strong messages to others. Some of these markings are easy to remove. Others, such as tattoos, are permanent.

You're Making It Up!

Actors use makeup when they want the expressions on their face to be seen clearly. Sometimes, certain features are made very big or important.

WINK!

Each clown has his or her own individual face-painted design. In Great Britain, clowns paint their design on an egg and register them so that they can't be copied.

◀ A clown will paint a large, smiling mouth to make the audience smile or feel happy.

◀ People often use makeup in everyday life too. The makeup may be saying "Look at my lips!," "Look in to my eyes!," or "Look at my lovely fingernails!"

Painted Bodies

A long time ago, warriors painted their faces and bodies to look more frightening. Some isolated tribes nowadays still use body paints for decoration. All over the world, children have fun with face paints and make themselves look like something else!

In South America, Arara Indians paint their bodies with designs which represent the fearsome jaguar. They believe this helps them with their hunting.

Talking Tattoos

Tattoos are permanent. They are designs marked on to the skin using a needle and colored inks. In Japan, some criminal gangs cover their whole bodies with tattoos to show which gang they belong to and that they are dangerous! But the **Maoris** of New Zealand used tattoos as a sign of importance. Today, most Maoris paint their faces on special occasions rather than have permanent tattoos. This man is painted like a chief!

Cracking the Code

It is important to notice other people's body language, and to learn how to use your own properly. Cracking the body language code can help you to understand people who may not speak your language. It can also help you make new friends!

Walk Tall

There are times when we can use body language to avoid trouble. Researchers have found that people who look confident are less likely to be bullied. Try it for yourself! Next time you feel that someone is being threatening, pull back your shoulders and look the other person straight in the eye. Keep your fear hidden.

Looking confident can fool a bully. They tend to seek out someone who looks weak—with shoulders slumped and eyes lowered.

I'm Nervous!

Do you feel nervous when you meet someone new? You can use your body language to help you! Start by smiling and saying hello. Or you could shake hands firmly. Make sure you maintain eye contact with the person you are meeting. Practice in front of a mirror. And remember, the other person is probably just as nervous as you!

Who's Lying?

If you are not telling the truth, be careful! Your body language might give you away. Someone who is hearing or telling lies might rest their fingers near the eyes, nose, mouth, or ears. They might avoid making eye contact, cross the legs, and fold the arms. But remember that body language is usually a group of signs together, not a single gesture. A finger on the nose may just be scratching an itch!

HELLO!
A carving of The Three Wise Monkeys first appeared in Japan in the 17th century. They have been used as a **symbol** of deceit ever since. Their body language shows that they see no evil, speak no evil, and hear no evil.

Calm Down!

How much notice do you take of the body language you use? If you find that you often upset or annoy people without meaning to, you may make a better impression by changing your body language.

Pointing a finger or balling the hands when you are speaking are two of the most irritating gestures.

Try opening up your hands and using the "palms up, palms down" positions instead. You will become a much more relaxing person to talk to!

Useful Words

Aboriginal: the Aboriginal people are the original inhabitants of Australia, who lived there for thousands of years before the arrival of European settlers in the 18th century.

adrenaline: a chemical produced by the body during times of stress, causing the heart to beat faster and raising blood pressure.

aggressive: describes behavior that offends or attacks others in the form of actions or words.

Bedouin: the nomadic people of the Arabian Desert in the Middle East. Nomadic people are people who do not live permanently in one place but move from time to time, usually in search of fresh pasture for their animals.

camouflage: use of shape or color to blend something in with its surroundings. Camouflage is usually a way of hiding from others.

canine teeth: the sharp pointed teeth found on either side of the mouth, between the front incisor teeth and the back molars, of meat-eating mammals.

Comanche: a Native American tribe from the southern United States.

confident: describes feeling sure or certain of oneself.

Darwin, Charles (1809-1892): an English naturalist famous for his theory of evolution. He gathered evidence to support his theory by sailing around the world on the *Beagle* from 1831-1836. In 1859 he published his findings in *Origin of Species*.

Deaf-dumb sign language: a language for deaf people first introduced in the 18th century by the French priest, Charles de L'Epée. It makes use of hand and arm movements and facial expression. Many deaf people also lip read. Each country has its own sign language and sign alphabet.

deceit: the act of making others believe something that is not true.

dialect: a different way of speaking the language of a country, usually found in different geographical regions. A dialect will have a distinctive accent and words which are not used elsewhere.

disguise: clothing or make-up worn for the purpose of hiding who one really is.

embarrassed: describes the feeling of being ashamed or uncomfortable about our behavior or appearance.

evolved: the process of evolution, where plants and animals have changed and adapted to their surroundings over very long periods of time.

gesture: a movement of the hands that suggests a certain mood, intention, or feeling.

involuntary: describes something that we do without choosing to do so, such as blinking, or a body movement that is a reflex action.

Maori: the original inhabitants of New Zealand before the coming of European settlers. The Maoris are descended from the Polynesian peoples of the South Pacific who settled in New Zealand about 700 years ago.

mime: a form of acting without words, where moods, ideas, or characters are suggested through gestures and movements only.

naïve: describes a person who is lacking experience with other people and the larger world. A naïve person is often too ready to believe whatever people say.

nectar: a sweet, sugary liquid produced by some flowers which is collected by bees and other insects for their food.

posture: the way in which a person positions or holds his or her body, especially the back, shoulders, and head.

predator: a meat-eating animal that hunts, or preys, on other animals for its food.

recruit: a new member of the armed forces.

species: a group of plants or animals of the same kind.

stereotyping: having a fixed idea of how a particular type of person should dress or behave.

symbol: a sign, shape, or object that represents something else, often a less concrete idea. For example, an owl is often seen as a symbol of wisdom.

tattoo: a permanent mark made on the body by pricking the skin with needles and applying colored inks and dyes. The process of tattooing can be very painful.

territory: an area regarded by a person or animal, or groups of the same, as being their home and property.

Tuareg: one of the nomadic peoples of the Sahara Desert in North Africa.

universal: describes something which applies to or is typical of everyone all over the world.

voicebox: found only in humans, the voicebox is the part of the air passage to the lungs containing the vocal cords which enable us to speak. The voicebox is also called the larynx.

Index